the little book of
MANIFESTING

First published in 2024 by OH
An Imprint of HEADLINE PUBLISHING GROUP

1

Disclaimer:

Cataloguing in Publication Data is available from the British Library

ISBN 978-1-03541-982-1

Compiled and written by: Katie Meegan
Editorial: Saneaah Muhammad
Designed and typeset in Joanna Sans Nova by: Stephen Cary
Project manager: Russell Porter
Production: Marion Storz
Printed and bound in China

Headline's policy is to use papers that are natural, renewable and recyclable products and made from wood grown in well-managed forests and other controlled sources. The logging and manufacturing processes are expected to conform to the environmental regulations of the country of origin.

HEADLINE PUBLISHING GROUP
An Hachette UK Company
Carmelite House, 50 Victoria Embankment, London EC4Y 0DZ

www.headline.co.uk   www.hachette.co.uk

the little book of
MANIFESTING

katie meegan

CONTENTS

Introduction   6

Chapter 1
About Manifesting   8

Chapter 2
Setting Your Intentions   34

Chapter 3
Visualization 101   52

Chapter 4
Raising Your Vibrations   74

Chapter 5
Co-Creating With the Universe 118

Chapter 6
Affirmations, Mantras
and Rituals   154

INTRODUCTION

What appears in your mind when you come across the word "manifesting"? Do you think of crystals, vision boards and signs from the spiritual realm? While all of these things have their place in a manifesting journey, manifesting is so much more than its signifiers.

Manifesting is, well, everything. It is carrying out the real inner work, addressing your limiting beliefs, your societal conditioning, your deepest fears and your most secret shames.

Manifesting is working towards a better version of your life, every day. Manifesting is embodying all that you hope to achieve, as if it's already happened. Manifesting is gratitude for all you already have, while humbly asking for more.

Manifesting is reprogramming negative subconscious beliefs that have been

holding you back for far too long. Manifesting is redirecting your energy towards what actually matters to you.

Manifesting is surrounding yourself with inspiration, hope and creativity. Manifesting is living in abundance. Manifesting is generosity of spirit and kindness to ourselves and others. Manifesting is detachment from material greed and all that not longer serves our higher purpose.

Manifesting is building a door, bit by bit, step by step, and then standing back and letting the universe turn the key.

Moreover, manifesting is now slowly becoming backed by hard evidence in the realms of neuroscience, quantum physics and psychology.

The universe has conspired for you to be here, right at this moment, reading these words. There is so much more in store for you than you can even conceive of.

So, that leaves us with just one question: Are you ready to start on your manifesting journey?

CHAPTER

1

ABOUT MANIFESTING

What is manifesting? While there are many answers to this question, at its very core, manifesting is redirecting desires into energy into action. The concept of manifestation has been around for thousands of years, and science is finally starting to catch up…

Manifestation means different things to many different people.

For the purposes of this book, we will continue with the following definition – courtesy of manifesting coach and writer, Roxie Nafousi.

"Manifesting is the ability to create the exact life that you want. It is the ability to draw in anything you desire and become the author of your own story. It looks and feels like magic, and we are all magicians."

Roxie Nafousi

Manifest: 7 Steps to Living Your Best Life, 2022.

The roots of manifestation can be found in religions and philosophies dating back thousands of years. Much of what we would now consider modern-day manifesting is derived from the Vedic scriptures of the Hindu tradition:

> *"Whatever world a man of pure understanding envisages in his mind and whatever desires he cherishes, that world he conquers and those desires he obtains."*

The Mundaka Upanishad

The ability to create our own reality can also be found in the Buddhist tradition:

"Whatever a monk keeps pursuing with his thinking and pondering, that becomes the inclination of his awareness."

Buddha (Dvedhavitakka Sutta)

While the idea of manifestation holds ancient roots, the contemporary incarnation of the ability to manifest a better life can be traced back to a nineteenth-century spiritual movement.

The New Thought school popularized spiritual healing and the term "creative visualization". The movement was not without its controversies, spreading the damaging belief that all illness was created in the mind. However, a lot of the language that the New Thought school popularized is still used today to teach manifestation, including a popular term: the Law of Attraction.

the law of attraction: the universal law that like attracts like.

The Law of Attraction concept re-entered twenty-first century popular discourse with the phenomenal success of Australian TV producer Rhonda Byrne's film and book, *The Secret*.

Widely regarded as repopularizing the Law of Attraction, Byrne's message was about the use of positive thinking to attract health, wealth, love and success.

"Life isn't happening to you, life is responding to you. You receive everything in your life based on what you've given."

Rhonda Byrne
The Secret, 2006.

Which brings us to today. In 2020, there was a 600% increase in Google searches regarding manifestation, and since the end of the COVID-19 pandemic, the interest in manifestation shows no sign of slowing down.

In an uncertain world, more and more people are turning to manifestation to create their dream life.

the SCIENCE of MANIFESTING

*"Imagination is everything.
It is the preview of
life's coming attractions."*

While manifesting can sometimes be
lumped in with other "new age fads",
emerging scientific studies have shown
that there is grounded scientific merit
in manifestation.

At its core, manifesting is the practice of positively engaging with the world around you and being hopeful for the future.

By practising manifestation, we cultivate a dispositional optimism or, put simply, a positive outlook on life whereby we generally expect the future to go well.

Having a positive outlook on life has now been linked to improved cardiovascular health, faster wound healing and even a slower spread of disease.

"The true gift of visualizing our intention again and again is to go through life with a buoyant sense that things will work out for us, which liberates us to be both responsive and resilient no matter what our external circumstances bring."

James R. Doty, MD
Mind Magic: The Neuroscience of Manifestation and How It Changes Everything, 2024.

The true magic of manifestation lies in the positive effect that the constant practice of manifestation has on the actual structure of our brains.

Recent research has shown that the practice of manifestation has a positive impact on the neuroplasticity of our brains.

NEUROPLASTICITY:

The brain's ability to change and adapt due to experience.

It is an umbrella term that refers to the brain's ability to change, reorganize or grow neural networks.

This can involve structural changes due to repeated actions and learning.

Imagine your brain as a series of paths in a forest.

The most well-worn paths, used everyday, are the clearest and most walked upon. However, when we create new habits, we veer off this well-trodden path and into the trees, creating new trails.

Through experience, repetition and intention, these new paths become our norm, enabling the brain to prune away the pre-existing negative patterns.

We have the power, through manifestation, to quite literally change the makeup of our brains.

By redirecting our attention in this way (e.g., walking down new trails) we create more grey matter (the good stuff) in the areas of the brain that help us to learn, perform and achieve any goal that we set our minds to.

With enough repetition, these neural pathways become embedded into our subconscious. We have more habits ingrained in our subconscious than we realize.

Think about making your morning coffee. There was a time, many years ago, when you had to actively focus on how to make your morning coffee, how many spoons to put in, whether to put in milk, cream, etc.

Now it's second nature – you can do it without even looking.

Think about driving to work. There would have been a time when the drive was new or unfamiliar, when you had to concentrate every step of the way.

Now, there are probably instances when you arrive at your destination without recalling the journey.

That's a pathway ingrained into your subconscious.

"*We are all manifesting the intentions stored within our minds in some form already in an untrained and uninformed way and the results are often haphazard, vague, and unfocused at best. To manifest consciously, we must reclaim our inner power to direct our attention.*"

James R. Doty, MD

Mind Magic: The Neuroscience of Manifestation and How It Changes Everything, 2024.

We have the power to change our minds at any moment. But what about changing the "universe" – the intangible energy and power that connects us all?

Science may have an answer for that too, in a rather unlikely place – quantum physics.

"As a man who has devoted his whole life to the most clearheaded science, to the study of matter, I can tell you as a result of my research about the atoms this much: There is no matter as such! All matter originates and exists only by virtue of a force, which brings the particles of an atom to vibration and holds this most minute solar system of the atom together... We must assume behind this force the existence of a conscious and intelligent Mind. This Mind is the matrix of all matter."

Max Planck

What we refer to as God, the universe or the infinite consciousness might actually be supported by quantum physics.

Various studies have shown that collective conscious attention can influence the world around us. One study showed that women who were prayed for had nearly twice the success in conceiving as women who weren't.

Another study comparing the progress of 22 injured bush babies (small primates) showed that the animals who were prayed for had a greater improvement in wound size than those that were not prayed for.

Whether you're swayed by the science or take comfort in the spiritual elements of manifestation, there is something in the practice of manifestation for everyone:

tapping into the infinite consciousness to influence the world around us, making our lives better or opening doors to our wildest dreams.

Throughout the following chapters, this infinite consciousness will be referred to as "the universe". If you prefer to read it within the context of your own pre-existing spiritual belief system, please feel free to do so.

*"Everything you want
is out there
waiting for you to ask."*

Jack Canfield

CHAPTER

2

SETTING
your
INTENTIONS

The first step in every manifestation journey is figuring out what you actually want to manifest! Or, in other words, setting your intentions. Our intentions must be as clear as possible in order for the universe to provide.

Before manifesting your dream future, you must acknowledge your present.

Imagine preparing for a long car journey. Do you simply just hop in the car and go? No – you gather belongings, adjust your mirrors and check if you have enough gas in the tank.

By taking some time to really assess where you are and where you have been, the universe will provide the answers of where you need to go next.

"The only difference between where you are and where you want to be is the steps you haven't taken yet."

Rigel Dawson

A common problem that new manifestors face is not knowing what to manifest.

Most begin their manifesting journey by knowing that they want something to change in their life but feel stuck or scared or unsure about how to make a change. Many come to manifestation at a time of life where they are in flux or facing a crossroads.

This may be difficult to hear, but the current version of you is exactly where you're meant to be at this moment.

Trust the journey.

the most important question in manifesting:

Know that this person you want to become, this higher self, already exists within you, patiently waiting to be released.

But first we must ask ourselves:

who am I now?

JOURNALLING EXERCISE 1:
CONNECTING with your PRESENT SELF

Using a journal, divide your page into eight categories:

family and friends: How satisfied are you with your relationships?

love and romantic relationships: If you are single, how satisfied are you with your dating experiences? If you're in a relationship, how satisfied are you with your partner?

health and wellbeing: Consider how you feel about your physical and mental wellbeing. Do you get enough sleep? Exercise? Healthy food?

self-development: Do you prioritize self-development through learning, reading, hobbies, travel or trying new things?

career: Are you happy in your current role? Is your workplace a positive environment?

money: Consider your incomings and outgoings. How do you feel about money?

environment: Consider your physical space, your home and who you share this space with.

spirituality: Are you living in alignment with your faith or spiritual practice?

Next, give each category an honest score between 1 and 10, with 1 being completely unfulfilled and 10 being the most fulfilled possible.

Don't worry about any low numbers, because they will guide you to the areas of life you need to change the most.

and remember...

ACKNOWLEDGMENT
is the **FIRST STEP**
of **CHANGE**

Now that we've pulled back the curtain on all areas of your life, we can uncover what really matters away from superficial trappings of success. Manifesting is not a material cheat, it is uncovering your truest purpose and living in alignment with this.

In order for the universe to provide, we must live in alignment with our purest and truest intentions.

In other words, we must embrace our true purpose.

JOURNALLING EXERCISE 2:
CONNECTING with your TRUE INTENTIONS

What is your purpose? Use these prompts and exmaples to guide you to connect with your inner being:

- What's a pasttime, hobby or skill you'd happily do for free?

    E.g., Gardening, playing an instrument, walking the dog, etc.

- What is something friends and family come to you for?

    E.g., Relationship advice, comfort, adventure, fixing household appliances, etc.

- Write about a time when you felt purposeful, fulfilled or accomplished.

  E.g., Supporting a loved one through a difficult time, learning something new, success on a work project, etc.

- How do I actually want to feel in my everyday life?

  E.g., Peaceful, content, energized, open, confident, etc.

- What are the values I want to live by? What actually matters the most to me?

    E.g., Family, health, spirituality, learning, etc.

- What are some signs I can feel in my mind and body when I am not engaging with something that is aligned with what I want?

    E.g., Sometimes the answer to what we do want lies in stripping away what we don't want.

Now that we have assessed where we are, we can turn our attention to who we wish to be, through visualization. Do not be despondent if your life is not where you want it to be at the moment.

The higher self – the dream self – is already within you. Manifesting will release them and set you on your higher path.

Now, we are ready to visualize our potential.

"You are what you want to become. Why search anymore? You are a wonderful manifestation. The whole universe has come together to make your existence possible."

Thich Nhat Hanh

CHAPTER

3

VISUALIZATION 101

When thinking of visualization,
it's tempting to think solely of a
colourful vision board. While there
is a place for lovely vision boards
(don't worry, we will be talking
about them later!), visualization is
so much more than that.

In order to align with the universe, you need to get specific, with it and yourself. It is key to use specificity in visualization.

Visualization is already used by countless celebrities, entrepreneurs and sport stars. Among the self-proclaimed fans of visualization are Oprah, Michael Phelps, Lewis Hamilton, Ariana Grande and Lady Gaga, to name just a few.

By visualizing the person we want to be, we tell our subconscious minds that this person is already within us, and our mind responds by altering our behaviour patterns.

It is by this altering of behaviour patterns that we are then able to pick up on the cues and signals around us that are sent from the universe.

How do we do this? By attracting desired emotion.

WE ATTRACT WHAT WE FEEL

Not only do we need to clearly *see* our desired future self, but we also need to clearly *feel* them.

Say, for example, that we want to manifest our dream home. We don't just manifest "our dream home" – we need to get specific with the universe.

Where is your dream home located? Which city? Which area? Which street? How many bedrooms does it have? Bathrooms? What does the carpet look like? The kitchen?

Now for the emotions. Try to be as specific as you can. Does your new home bring you comfort? Contentment? Peace? Joy? Creativity? What's coming up for you?

No two journeys are the same, so it is important to really sink into your intuition and see what represents itself.

Read on for visualization techniques to apply to your everyday life.

VISUALIZATION MEDITATION:

step-by-step

1 Find somewhere quiet and comfortable to sit or lie down. Close your eyes.

2 Take ten deep breaths, in through your nose, filling up your belly, and out through your mouth with a sigh.

3 Focus on an image of your highest self. What are you doing? What are you wearing? What can you hear? What are you smelling? What can you taste?

4 Associate with the image. Can you go into your higher self? Can you view your life through your own eyes instead of from outside of your body? Do your emotions feel stronger?

5 Focus on the feelings attached to your highest self. How do you feel? Where in your body do you feel that emotion? Notice how your energy shifts.

6 Slowly come back to the present moment, keep the energy of your higher self flowing or write a few words in your journal about how you feel.

SCRIPT YOUR IDEAL DAY

Scripting is a manifestation technique whereby we write our day out as if our manifestation has already occurred.

Writing in the present tense (as opposed to the future) creates the energy we want to put out into the universe to attract these very things.

This is also a great technique to use if you feel overwhelmed with the amount of opportunities you wish to manifest.

Take your journal and script your perfect day in the present tense. Use the prompts on the next page to get started.

- When do you wake up? Where do you wake up? Is there anyone beside you?

- What is your morning routine? What do you eat for breakfast? What does your home look like? What does it feel like?

- What is your self-care routine?

- Where do you work? What work are you doing? How does that make you feel?

- Who do you meet throughout the day? How do those interactions make you feel?

- What does your evening routine include? How do you feel just before you fall asleep?

RIFF WITH A FRIEND

To riff is to improvise out loud, like in jazz music. Sitting with a trusted friend, tell each other about your manifestations as if they're already happening.

Perhaps you describe how your new business is going, perhaps they describe an amazing date they've been on, perhaps you both describe an amazing trip that you want to take together.

The possibilities are endless!

It may feel unnatural at first, but remember, we did this as children all the time when playing pretend!

Imagining your highest self and best life with a friend will add fun and increase your positive energy. Additionally, speaking your manifestations out loud is powerful.

It shows the universe that you are ready to embrace your highest self.

WRITE A LETTER AS YOUR FUTURE SELF

Visualize yourself a year from now, five years from now, 10 years from now.

Write a letter from the perspective of your future self writing to your current self. Tell yourself what has happened in that time, all the positive changes you've made, all the goals you've achieved. Tell yourself what you need to do in the next year.

Date the letter and store it somewhere safe. Set a reminder on your phone to look at it again after that amount of time has passed (the amount of time between now and your future self).

You already know, subconsciously, what changes you need to make in your life – by writing as if you've already done them, you're rewiring your brain to believe that these goals are possible.

Not only possible, but achievable.

ACTING AS IF

Also known as "fake it until you make it"! Acting as if is also a technique used in cognitive behavioural therapy (CBT), which teaches that changing our behaviour can change our thoughts.

This is also known as the outside–in approach, by changing your external environment to reflect the positive changes you want to make internally.

For example, if you want to start a business, act as if you are already a successful entrepreneur. What would a day in the life of that person look like? What routines do they have? What systems have they put in place?

Or, if you want to be healthier, make the choices of that healthy person who you wish to be. For example, you're not starting a new gym routine, you already have a fulfilling gym routine.

At every opportunity, ask yourself, "would this version of me do that?"

VISION BOARDING 101

We promised you that get to them! Vision boards are the physical and visual representation of your dream life. Follow the steps below to make the most of your vision board:

step 1: get the mood right

Light some candles, clear your space and allow fresh air or burn some incense to cleanse the space. Make an event of creating your moodboard.

step 2: get prepping

Before we come to the fun bit of cutting out images, we need to do some work.

Take a blank sheet of paper and write a date at the top. This could be one, five or even 10 years into the future.

If you seek more guidance on your visions, separate your life into categories: personal growth, love and romance, career, friends and family, house/home and hobbies/leisure.

step 3: get in the visualization zone

Pause for a moment and take a few deep breaths, embodying the feelings of your future self. Think about where you want to be in the future.

You can ask yourself the following questions:

How do I feel about my future self?

Who surrounds me?

Where do I live?

What is my career?

What have I changed in my life?

What am I most proud of?

Write down your answers freely, without editing or judging them.

step 4: get manifesting

Write down what you want to manifest or cut out images and words that resonate with your goals.

Have fun with this part, and enjoy the creativity of this process!

step 5: display it, or don't...

Some manifesting gurus encourage you to display your vision board where you can see it everyday.

Others, however, advise you to put it away and return to it on the date that you wrote down. Do what works best for you.

Don't have the space for a traditional vision board? Create a digital collage and save it as your phone's screensaver.

"Once your mind gets organized, the way you think is the way you feel – so your emotion will also get organized. Once your thought and emotion are organized, your energies will get organized in the same direction. Once your thought, emotion and energies are organized, your very body will also get organized. Once all these four are organized in one direction, your ability to create and manifest what you want is phenomenal."

Sadhguru

CHAPTER

4

RAISING
your
VIBRATIONS

Now that we are clear about what we wish to manifest, we must raise our vibrations to meet the universe at where we need to be. We do this by addressing our limiting beliefs, cultivating self-love and living with an abundance mindset.

Have you ever had a day where just everything seems to go wrong?

You sleep through your alarm, your toast is burnt, your train is delayed, you have a bad day at work, it's raining. One thing just snowballs into the next and the next, until you're just ready for the day to be over.

On the other hand, have you ever had a fantastic day where just everything seems to fall perfectly into place?

This is due to the Law of Attraction, as we mentioned in chapter 1, and its big sister, the Law of Vibration.

the law of attraction states that like attracts like.

the law of vibration states that all living objects are vibrating at different speeds, emitting various frequencies. How we attune to these frequencies affects how we attract our desires.

"Quantum physics, the most tested, verified and truthful of all the sciences, emphasizes that consciousness creates our life experiences. Consequently, by reprogramming consciousness, we are empowered to take control of our creation and manifest a life we might characterize as 'Heaven-on-Earth'."

Dr. Bruce Lipton

As humans, we sense energy all the time. Have you ever met someone that you instantly felt uneasy with? Or vice versa, being in a crowded room but being drawn to a certain person? That's the meeting of energies.

In order to manifest, we must be in a high-vibrational state. But how do we get there?

By first addressing our limiting beliefs.

LIMITING BELIEFS

Every single one of us has limiting beliefs. A limiting belief is a negative thought that has been repeated so many times that it becomes subconscious.

Limiting beliefs are rooted in the lowest vibrational energy forms: shame, guilt, insecurity or even anger. Most, if not all, limiting beliefs begin in childhood. It is not only those who experienced early childhood trauma or neglect that internalize limiting beliefs. Even those raised in the most loving of homes can absorb negative subconscious messaging from friends, teachers or even society at large.

Limiting beliefs can sound like this:

*My brother's the high-achieving one,
I'm the family failure.*

I'm terrible with money, I'm always in debt.

*I'll never find a partner, they always let
me down.*

I can never stick to a gym routine.

*I could never start my own business, it would
fail and I'd be humiliated.*

*I can't move to a different country, what if
I hate it and have to return home?*

*I'm too stupid to go back to higher
education, I sucked at school.*

Do any of those limiting beliefs sound familiar? Sit with the emotions these thoughts bring up, where do you feel them in the body?

The good news is that it is never too late to rewire your brain and let go of these limiting beliefs. You have the ability, through neuroplasticity (see page 23), to create new pathways in your brain, new positive messaging and new beliefs.

You deserve to let go of all that no longer serves your higher purpose.

"*To manifest anything into your life, and to do so effortlessly and effectively, you must believe that you are worthy of having it.*"

Roxie Nafousi

CHALLENGING LIMITING BELIEFS

For every manifestation, we must also interrogate the limiting beliefs that are attached to it.

This is not a magic cure that provides instant healing – you will need to return to these steps repeatedly as these negative conditioned patterns occur throughout your journey.

This won't be easy.

This is the hard work that shows the universe that we are ready to show up and receive the blessings it has planned for you.

step 1: acknowledge your limiting beliefs

Say, for example, you want to open a bakery. But you're scared to leave your stable 9–5 job and the financial security that it provides. You're worried that people will judge you for wanting to do your own thing. You're scared of failure, of letting people down.

In a journal, write down every single fear or doubt you have about the manifestation. Ask yourself, what is the "worst possible scenario"?

step 2: challenge yourself

For every fear or doubt listed, ask yourself these questions:

Is it a fact or is it a belief?

Have I always thought in this way?

Where does this belief come from?

How is this belief holding me back?

step 3: argue for and against

This is where we test the validity of your held beliefs. It may seem counterintuitive to back up your fears and doubts, but once you do this you're able to see how tightly you've been holding on to them. For example:

argument for: It will fail because I'm not a great baker, I don't even know enough about cake decorating to start a bakery.

argument against: My family and friends are always complimenting my baking. And I can attend a cake decorating course to hone my skills.

Repeat this step for each of the negative statements you wrote down.

step 4: create a new belief

By arguing against your limiting belief you are already reframing your thinking. Decide how you want to feel and honour it. Write down your new belief and repeat it daily as an affirmation or a mantra until it feels natural (for more on affirmations, see page 154).

Now you are ready to take action! Return to this exercise as many times as you need whenever old negative thought patterns reappear.

Challenge those limiting beliefs with your newly formed positive affirmations. You've got this!

LIMITING BELIEFS and RELATIONSHIPS

As we've seen so far, limiting beliefs don't come from nowhere. Now that you've interrogated your limiting beliefs, it is time to assess how those around you raise or lower your vibrational energy.

Pay attention to how you feel after interacting with friends and family, work colleagues and those around you.

Do you feel drained, buoyant, peaceful, resentful? Perhaps you need to speak to a therapist about your relationship dynamics, set boundaries with loved ones or communicate your needs more directly.

Identify those around you who are "energy expanders": Those who inspire you and feed into your dreams and ambitions. This could be someone in your friendship circle, a colleague or even someone who you follow online.

Mindfully curate your social feeds to include people who are already successful in your field, for inspiration.

CULTIVATING SELF-LOVE

Without self-love, there cannot be a successful manifestation.

Self-love tells the universe:

"I am ready, I am willing, I am worthy of the greatness you choose to bestow upon me."

Small acts of daily self-love and self-care raise our vibrations.

There are countless ways to practise self-love, from drinking more water to leaving a bad relationship. Every minute of every day is an opportunity to practise self-discipline, self-love and self-respect.

If we've been stuck in patterns of self-sabotage for years, or even decades, it will take a lot of work to undo this damage to your self-esteem. Ask a trusted family member, friends or a therapist for support on this journey.

Self-love starts small – it can begin with little acts that we incorporate into our daily routine.

daily acts of self-care

- Listen to your favourite happy song
- Open your window and let in fresh air
- Block/unfriend negative pages and people
- Make a delicious and healthy meal
- Journal
- Meditate
- Go for a walk in nature
- Call a friend for a chat

- Declutter your space
- Try a new coffee spot
- Light a candle
- Prioritise getting 8–10 hours of quality sleep
- Cancel plans
- Add plants to your space
- Watch a funny or hopeful film
- Dance
- Practise a musical instrument for fun
- Meditate

- Paint or draw
- Listen to an inspiring podcast
- Take a long shower or bath
- Read a book
- Practise yoga
- Volunteer
- Donate old clothing
- Practise gratitude (see page 106)
- Drink some water
- Sit in the sunlight

- Create a skincare routine
- Add essential oils to your home
- Enjoy some quiet time
- Eat a nourishing breakfast
- Put your phone to the side for a while
- Bake something yummy

CHALLENGING NEGATIVE THOUGHTS

You have the choice to challenge every negative thought that you experience.

Again, this will take practise but start by catching yourself the next time you think negatively about yourself, your body, your ability or your situation. Take the following examples:

"What if it doesn't work out?"
What if it does?

"I am not good enough."
I am where I am meant to be at this moment.

"I do not know how."
I can learn how to.

"It's going to be too much work."
I can handle any obstacle that comes my way.

ABUNDANCE verses LACK MINDSET

It's time to talk about the green-eyed monster: envy. Jealousy is an emotion very few of us want to admit to feeling but nearly everyone has felt it.

Think about the last time you felt a pang of jealousy. Was it while scrolling through Instagram and seeing an influencer on a glamorous holiday? Did your friend get that promotion you were working so hard for? Do you wish you had your sister's new car?

Jealousy can also present itself in another form: judgement. We, as a society, love to judge others.

Think about the last time you caught yourself judging someone. Was it someone in an eye-catching outfit? Was it someone promoting their side-hustle online? Perhaps it was someone who always speaks up for themselves at work.

Think about where this judgement is coming from. Are you actually envious of their confidence, their drive, their self-assuredness?

Reframe your judgments.

Jealousy, envy and judgement are all low-vibrational emotions. They keep us stuck in a comparison loop.

By envying others we are saying to the universe:

> *"I do not believe that there is enough love, success, wealth or opportunities for me."*

This is the **lack mindset**, also known as the fixed mindset or scarcity mindset.

"*Whether you believe you can do a thing or not, you are right.*"

Henry Ford

The opposite of the lack mindset is the **abundance mindset**. An abundant mindset is the belief that there is enough wealth, happiness and success for all.

- A **lack mindset** focuses on never having enough.
- An **abundant mindset** knows that there is always enough to go around.

- A **lack mindset** non-constructively criticizes others.
- An **abundant mindset** offers appreciation for efforts and embraces teamwork.

- A **lack mindset** avoids pitfalls and is risk averse.
- An **abundant mindset** sees opportunity to overcome challenges and learn from mistakes.

Take an honest look at your thought patterns – where do you spend most of your time and energy – on the lack side or on the abundance side?

As with the Law of Attraction, like attracts like. By embracing the abundance mindset we are telling the universe that we are open to good things coming our way.

There is a common misconception that "abundance" applies only to material riches.

But the truth is, to be truly abundant means to be rich in every area of life. Rich in relationships. Rich in health. Rich in peace. Rich in purpose. Rich in alignment.

This is the true meaning of abundance.

"The more you praise and celebrate your life, the more there is in life to celebrate."

Oprah Winfrey

GRATITUDE

Gratitude is one of the highest-vibration emotions there is, and it is key to the manifesting journey.

Read on to discover the power of gratitude, and how to incorporate gratitude into your life.

gratitude

The quality of being thankful; readiness to show appreciation for and to return kindness.

The Oxford English Dictionary.

Let's face it, it is nearly impossible to stay in the vibration of joy, abundance and happiness every single moment of our lives.

Even our low-vibration emotions have a place – we need to have the full spectrum of emotions in order to be grateful for what we have. Living in a state of gratitude can be adopted on even our most challenging days.

Gratitude is one of the most powerful tools that we as manifestors have at our disposal.

"Gratitude is the ability to experience life as a gift. It liberates us from the prison of self-preoccupation."

John Ortberg

three types of gratitude

There are three categories of gratitude that can override any difficult low-vibration emotion. Please see some examples below. Can you think of more gratitudes to add to each category?

gratitude for yourself: These are traits that you admire about yourself.

> *I am grateful for my resilience. I am grateful for my health. I am grateful for my work ethic. I am grateful for all that I have overcome.*

gratitude for your life: These are the external things in your life that you appreciate.

> *I am grateful for my family and friends. I am grateful for my opportunities. I am grateful for my home. I am grateful for the food in my fridge and safe running water from my tap.*

gratitude for the world: These are universal to all (this is a particularly good category to focus on when your own life or negative emotions feel overwhelming).

> *I am grateful for puppies and kittens. I am grateful for music. I am grateful for connection between people. I am grateful for spring flowers and autumn leaves.*

Try adding your own gratitudes to the categories on the previous page.

Notice how your body reacts to the feeling of gratitude.

As well as relaxing us, gratitude instantly raises our vibrations, making us unconsciously smile and instantly feel calmer.

The practice of gratitude is so powerful that it has been proven to have physiological benefits. According to Dr Joe Dispenza, the practice of gratitude, appreciation or kindness for just 9–10 minutes, three times a day, four days a week can actually strengthen your immune system by roughly 50%.

i'll-be-happy-when-itis

We're all guilty of it. How many times have you thought:

"I'll be happy when I get that job/ house/partner/handbag"?

By pushing away our happiness on to some arbitrary future point we are telling the universe that we are ungrateful for what we currently have, that we are not prepared for the opportunities it's lining up for us.

Embrace gratitude in the present.

GRATITUDE JOURNALLING

While gratitude can, and should, be practised at any time of the day or night, journalling is also a fantastic way to tap into those high vibrations.

Every morning, or every evening, or both, write down 15 things that you're grateful for. Feel free to choose five things in the three categories on pages 110–111. Keep your gratitude journal near to your bed to develop the habit of connecting this gratitude list to your pre-sleep routine.

POSITIVITY JOURNALLING

This is a broader form of gratitude journalling. Before you go to sleep, take 5–10 minutes to note down every single good thing that happened in your day. Yes, everything. If your bus was on time, if the weather was pleasant, if you grabbed lunch in your favourite spot, if you had a nice chat with your neighbour.

You'll be surprised to see how many positive moments go by in the day without us noticing them.

thank you, more please

For some, it can feel rather counterintuitive to be so grateful for our present lives when we want to manifest for more in the future. You might ask, "How am I supposed to be so grateful for my tiny apartment when I'm manifesting my dream house? How am I supposed to be grateful for my unfulfilling job while I'm manifesting my dream career?"

The attitude of gratitude tells the universe:

Thank you, more please.

While you can sit in abundance and gratitude, you can absolutely desire more from life. Be grateful to yourself for the aligned action that you're taking to achieve those goals.

CHAPTER

5

CO-CREATING
with the
UNIVERSE

Manifesting your dream life is going to require work. We can't just sit back and expect it all to fall into our laps. Build the door so the universe can provide the key.

"Manifesting isn't about getting; it's about becoming."

Gabby Bernstein

Manifestation is not passive. You cannot simply make a vision board and wait for your goals and opportunities to appear.

Manifesting is the creative process of aligning with the energy of the universe to co-create an experience that elevates you to your higher self.

Take, for example, manifesting a year-long backpacking trip. You can start by breaking down the costs of how much such a trip would cost, then creating a savings plan to work towards that goal.

Keep the feelings you want to manifest alive by bookmarking locations you want to go, saving inspiring content, perhaps buying a travel guide about the country you're going to.

Or imagine manifesting passing exams with good grades. This won't come to fruition without dedicating time and effort to studying.

By showing the universe that you're willing to work with it, you're co-creating with the life you're meant to live.

This is also called **inspired action** or aligned action.

That's all well and good, but how does inspired action differ from any old goal-setting technique?

As manifesting coach Victoria Jackson writes:

> *"While action in the traditional sense is results-led and solution-focused, inspired action is more connected to a strong inner urge to do something related to the vision of your dream life."*

Manifesting for Beginners:
A Step-by-step Guide to Attracting A Life You Love, 2022.

Taking inspired action can feel like a risk. It's so easy to predict the worst possible outcomes, but these rarely, if ever, come true.

Inspired action involves stepping out of your comfort zone with sacrifice, determination and consistency. Even on the hardest days you should always be able to return to your vision, your why and look at your vision board and know that you are showing up for yourself.

However, what do we do if we're worried that we're on the wrong path? Working toward the wrong things? How do we tell the difference between fear-based quitting and relinquishing to the universe?

The answer is intuition.

LISTENING
to your
INTUITION

Picture this: you have an idea to move your life forward, perhaps it's moving to a different city.

You quit your job, you start to pack your bags, but as the day of departure approaches, something just doesn't feel right.

Is it fear, a limiting belief rearing its ugly head? Or is it the universe, nudging you in a different direction?

A common question manifesters ask is how to know the difference between a fear-based decision and an intuition-led one.

We identify this difference by tapping into our very own intuition.

"*Have the courage to follow your heart and intuition. They somehow already know what you truly want to become. Everything else is secondary.*"

Steve Jobs

meditation for intuition

- Sit or lie down in a comfortable place. Keep a pen and journal within easy reach.

- Take 10 deep breathes, in through your nose and out through your mouth.

- In your mind's eye, scan through your body, starting at your toes. Send loving white light to your toes, your feet, your ankles, slowly raising upwards throughout the rest of your body.

- Every time you feel your mind wander, gently, and without judgement, guide it back to the last body part you can recall.

- Complete the scan until you reach between your eyebrows. This is where your third eye sits. Pause here for 10 breaths, picturing a clear white light beaming out from your third eye.

- Bring this light inward and down into your gut. Pause here for 10 breaths.

- Ask the universe for guidance.

- Stay here for as long as you need. As you slowly wake up, grab your journal to note down – without limitations or judgement – any thoughts or sensations that occurred.

*"Fake it
until you become it."*

Unknown

Now that we've addressed how to tell if your intuition is guiding you rather than expressing fear, doubt and limiting beliefs, we must make a conscious commitment to accept discomfort.

In order to stop ourselves from slipping back into old patterns, we must learn to live in our empowered state until it feels natural.

Until that happens, you've got to fake it until you make it.

A technique for embodying your best self when it all feels a bit overwhelming is creating an alter-ego for the traits you wish to embody.

An excellent example of this is Beyoncé and her famous alter-ego, Sasha Fierce. While her music transitioned from polished pop to a sexier R'n'B sound, Beyoncé found it difficult to step into the confidence that her new music required.

And thus, Sasha Fierce was born.

Speaking to Oprah in 2008, Beyoncé explained:

"Sasha Fierce appears, and my posture and the way I speak and everything is different."

However, just two years later, the superstar told *Allure* magazine that she had "killed" Sasha Fierce:

"I don't need Sasha Fierce anymore, because I've grown and now I'm able to merge the two."

What does your Sasha Fierce look like? Are they in alignment with your highest self? Can you embody them when the universe presents you with opportunities to step into your power?

"*What we put into the Universe, we get back like an echo.*"

Abraham Hicks

In the words of Yoda:

> *"Do or do not, there is no try."*

The universe does not accept aimless attempts. If you truly believe that you are worthy of your wildest dreams, you need to show the universe as much. Even when the universe throws obstacles in your way.

OBSTACLES
and
SETBACKS

You will (not might, will) encounter obstacles on your manifesting journey.

Whether it's a toxic relationship, a job gone wrong or an opportunity missed, remember that the universe has your back through every scenario.

In your manifesting journey, and in life in general, you will experience disappointment, rejection, heartbreak and grief.

While manifesting involves hope for a better life and alignment with your higher self, the universe may put tests and obstacles in your way, to determine if you're truly ready to receive your dreams.

For example, you want to manifest your dream partner, but suddenly a past partner reappears in your life.

It is easy to fall back into comfortable and familiar patterns and then blame ourselves when it doesn't work out for the best.

Does this mean that you've failed in your manifestation? Absolutely not. The universe is always on your side. Even when we do not live in alignment with our best selves or stray from our intuition, you always have the ability to choose your next steps and learn from your mistakes.

There are countless stories of actors and singers going to just one more audition before giving up. Or dream houses falling through only for a better one to appear in time. Or finding "one" just as you've stopped looking. Or not getting an interview for that dream job you manifested only to get a much better position.

When you follow your intuition, do the work and keep your belief – the universe will show up when the timing is exactly right.

The universe only ever has three answers to your manifestations:

yes

not yet

I have something better in store

When things don't go your way, you are actually being given the greatest opportunity to show up for yourself, to build resilience and inner strength and to learn valuable lessons.

You can always choose. Do you choose to lose faith in yourself or do you choose to trust that the universe has something better in store for you?

"We want solutions, but what we really need are attitudes.
You don't need abs, but rather an attitude of training. You don't need the answer, but rather an attitude of curiosity. You don't need an easier life, but rather an attitude of perseverance.
Attitude precedes outcome."

James Clear.

LETTING GO

This is another facet of manifestation that may seem counterintuitive at first: **letting go of the outcome**.

You have to be at peace with the fact that your manifestation may not come to fruition in the way that you imagined it, in the way that you longed for it.

Really interrogate yourself: Will you truly be happy if your dreams don't manifest in the exact way you desire?

If so, you need to release control to the universe.

Fully releasing control to the universe is being at peace with your life path, regardless of the direction.

It is trusting that as you are living in alignment and working with your intuition, the universe is unfolding as it should. This could be particularly difficult if you are emotionally attached to the outcome, for example, manifesting starting a family, finding love or better health.

Be kind to yourself.

The manifestation is in the emotion, not in the material gain.

For example, you wanted to manifest a certain amount of money into your bank account within a year. So you take a highly stressful job that pays well, you save every penny and work extra hours so you do not have the capacity to see loved ones, causing some relationships to drift. At the end of the year, you have reached your monetary goal. But do you feel satisfied? Perhaps briefly.

More likely, you are stressed, burned-out and feeling isolated from family and friends. Your job is too demanding to really enjoy those luxury holidays you were planning.

Now backtrack to your original manifestation.

When you were manifesting the money, what energies and emotions were attaching themselves to that visualization? Was it comfort? Security? Freedom? Independence?

If you had taken a lower-paying job, you may not have reached that million-pound mark, but maybe you would have had more time to spend with loved ones, be more present and focus on the abundance already in your life. This is what we mean when we say that the universe has a better plan for you.

Let go of the outcome. Trust the process.

JOURNAL PROMPTS
for LETTING GO

Relinquishing control to the universe is far easier said than done.

If you struggle with this aspect, know that you are not alone. Interrogate what limiting beliefs are keeping you in this scarcity mindset or use these journal prompts to guide your exploration:

- What is holding you back from relinquishing control to the universe?

- Why are you worrying about your manifestation not coming to fruition right away?

- What could bring contentment and calmness to your energy right now?

- Can you name a time where a disappointment actually gave way to a better opportunity?

Do you feel ready now to co-create with the universe? You may feel like you're standing at the bottom of a mountain, overwhelmed at the thought of all that is ahead of you. Just remember:

YOU CONTROL YOUR THOUGHTS.

TAKE ONE STEP AT A TIME.

THERE IS ALWAYS
OPPORTUNITY IN SETBACKS.

THE UNIVERSE HAS YOUR BACK.

THE VIEW FROM THE TOP IS
WORTH IT.

CHAPTER

6

AFFIRMATIONS, MANTRAS and RITUALS

The daily practice of affirmation and incorporating mantras into your spiritual practice is key to resetting your thought patterns, raising your vibrations and ultimately attracting all that you deserve. Read on to learn about incorporating all this, and more, into your day-to-day life.

how affirmations work

Affirmations promote self-confidence and belief in your ability to manifest your goals. Words of affirmation are designed to challenge our automatic negative thought patterns. Essentially, an affirmation, when attached to emotion and repeated consistently, should replace an old, unhelpful or limiting belief within your subconscious. This is due to the connection formed in the brain through neuroplasticity (see page 23).

Affirmations can boost your self-esteem and vibrations. They can help you to bring a feeling of closure to an event or relationship. They can provide you with confidence, clarity and contentment.

When beginning this practice of positive self-talk, we need to feel like the affirmations are realistic.

For example, if you suffer from poor body image, saying, **"I love how I look in every picture taken of me"** would not align with where you are on your journey.

Instead, you could change it to **"I appreciate all the ways in which my body keeps me alive throughout the day."**

Meet yourself where you are.

AFFIRMATION RITUALS

Just as with meditation, there is no one-stop shop when it comes to incorporating affirmations into your life.

Most coaches and guides recommend doing your affirmations in the morning, when your brain is the most receptive, and to start your day off with some positive energy.

There is only one real rule to manifesting affirmations: always use the present tense. This not only programmes your subconscious, but also indicates to the universe that you are in an abundance mindset and ready to receive its blessings.

Either speak aloud or write down your affirmations. They can remain private to you, but the energy needs to be released into the universe.

Just some ideas of where you can practise affirmations:

- **In front of a mirror, spoken aloud.**

- **While making your morning cup of coffee.**

- **Written in your journal.**

- **In bed before going to sleep.**

Turn the page to view affirmations for all areas of life to get you started.

Choose between three and five from any category you feel most aligned with, and practise them for a week.

affirmations for self-love

1. I love and accept myself unconditionally.

2. I am enough exactly as I am.

3. I radiate self-confidence and self-respect.

4. I am deserving of love and respect from myself and others.

5. My self-worth is not determined by others.

6. I am proud of who I am and who I am becoming.

7. I honour my body and treat myself with kindness.

8. I trust myself and my intuition.

9. I am a unique and valuable person.

10. I forgive myself and release myself from any past mistakes

affirmations for romantic relationships

1. I am worthy of a loving and healthy relationship.

2. I attract a partner who respects and cherishes me.

3. My heart is open to giving and receiving love.

4. I deserve a partner who loves and supports me.

5. Love flows to me effortlessly and abundantly.

6. I am in a loving, committed relationship.

7. My relationship is filled with trust, respect and joy.

8. I attract love that feels right to my soul.

9. I am grateful for the love and affection in my life.

10. I radiate love and attract love in return.

affirmations for finding your purpose

1. I am in alignment with my true purpose.
2. I am open to discovering my unique gifts and talents.
3. My life is filled with passion and purpose.
4. I am guided towards my highest good.
5. I trust that I am on the right path.
6. I am dedicated to pursuing my dreams and goals.
7. My purpose is unfolding before me every day.
8. I am making a positive impact in the world.
9. I am confident in my ability to fulfil my purpose.
10. I am grateful for the clarity and direction in my life.

affirmations for financial abundance

1. I am a magnet for financial abundance.

2. Money flows to me easily and effortlessly.

3. I am open to receiving all the wealth life offers me.

4. I am financially free and secure.

5. I am grateful for the money I have and the money that is on its way.

6. I deserve to be prosperous and successful.

7. My income is constantly increasing.

8. I manage my money wisely and efficiently.

9. I attract opportunities to create wealth.

10. I am financially abundant and prosperous.

affirmations for career

1. I am successful in my career and passionate about my work.

2. I attract opportunities that align with my career goals.

3. My skills and talents are recognized and rewarded.

4. I am open to new and exciting career prospects.

5. I am confident in my professional abilities.

6. My career is fulfilling and brings me joy.

7. I am making meaningful contributions to my field.

8. I am continually growing and advancing in my career.

9. I am appreciated and respected in my workplace.

10. I am achieving my career goals and aspirations.

affirmations for friends, family and community

1. I am surrounded by loving and supportive friends and family.

2. I attract positive and uplifting relationships.

3. I am a good friend and value my friendships.

4. My family relationships are harmonious and loving.

5. I contribute to my community in meaningful ways.

6. I am grateful for the love and support of my friends and family.

7. I attract people who enrich my life.

8. I am an important and valued member of my community.

9. I nurture my relationships with love and care.

10. I am open to forming new, positive connections.

affirmations for your living space

1. My home is a sanctuary of happiness.

2. I am grateful for my beautiful and comfortable home.

3. I have a home that meets all my needs and desires.

4. My home is filled with love and positive energy.

5. I create a safe and nurturing environment for myself and my family.

6. I feel at ease in my home.

7. My home is a reflection of my inner peace.

8. I am constantly improving and beautifying my living space.

9. I attract abundance and prosperity into my home.

10. I am grateful for the roof over my head and the warmth it provides.

affirmations for travel and hobbies

1. I am open to exploring new experiences.

2. I attract opportunities for adventure.

3. I am grateful for the time and resources that allow me to enjoy my hobbies.

4. My life is filled with exciting travel and leisure activities.

5. I am passionate about my hobbies and pursue them with joy.

6. I attract opportunities to learn and grow through travel.

7. My leisure time is fulfilling and rejuvenating.

8. I create beautiful memories through my travels and hobbies.

9. I am open to meeting new people and experiencing new cultures.

10. I am grateful for the fun in my life.

MANTRAS

A mantra or mantram, in the Hindu and Buddist traditions, is a sacred utterance, a sound, a syllable, word or a group of words believed by practitioners to have spiritual powers or potency.

The energetic form of a mantra is a repeated word or sound that aids concentration in meditation and visualization.

Today, the word "mantra" has been co-opted into common speech to represent a statement or slogan that is frequently repeated. But what do mantras have to do with manifestation?

Mantras help us to move deeper into a meditative experience, using the vibration of sound and words to sharpen focus, linking the emotions and visualization you associate with your higher self to the vibrational frequencies you wish to attract.

Mantras can also expel any negative energy, clearing your path to take aligned action.

In some spiritual traditions, "Om" is believed to represent the sound of the universe.

The "Om" mantra is made of three syllables: A-U-M. Each syllable represents a different universal aspect:

"A" represents creation.

"U" represents preservation.

"M" represents ending.

Connected, they represent the circle of life and the universal flow of energy.

When chanting the "Om" mantra, you are tapping into the universal energy.

This vibration resonates throughout your body and mind, calming stress and focusing your thoughts.

When you are in this open state, you are more attractive to the positive energy that the universe is sending your way.

om mantra meditation for manifestation

step 1: Find a comfortable place to sit. Sit upright in a chair with your hands resting on your knees or on the floor in a cross-legged position with your hands resting on your lap. Close your eyes.

step 2: Take deep breaths, in through your nose, into your belly and out through your mouth. Repeat this until the breaths become long and deep.

step 3: Now direct your attention to your mouth. Start moving your lips and mouth and repeat all the vowel sounds - "A, E, I, O, U" - aloud. This is to relax the jaw and loosen your facial muscles.

step 4: Keep your focus and gently open your eyes, keeping your attention on a point in the middle distance. Take a deep breath in and sound the "Om" aloud. As one mantra fades out, pause, take another deep breath in and repeat at least five times.

step 5: As the vibrations flow through your chest, throat, mouth and space, imbue them with the energy of your manifestation and higher self.

step 6: Finish your mantra practice with some affirmations, breathing exercises or gratitude journalling.

MANIFESTING RITUALS

While manifesting is an ongoing process, we can incorporate rituals into our day, week or month to clear our energies and attract the life we desire.

By showing up and committing to your higher self, the universe will respond.

daily morning ritual: gratitude and affirmation

step 1: Upon waking up, sit comfortably and take three deep breaths.

step 2: Think of up to 15 things you're grateful for. Feel the gratitude for a new day deeply (see page 106 for more gratitude practices).

step 3: Repeat positive affirmations related to your goals (see page 154 for affirmations).

step 4: Visualize your day going as well as you could hope for. See yourself taking aligned action and feel the emotions associated with stepping into your power.

daily evening ritual: reflection and release

step 1: Before bed, find a quiet space and sit comfortably. Turn off all distractions.

step 2: Reflect on your day. Think about what went well and what you could improve.

step 3: Write down three things you achieved or are proud of (see page 116 for a positivity journalling exercise).

step 4: Write down any negative thoughts or experiences that you want to release. After writing, take a moment to visualize letting go of these negativities.

Be honest with yourself but do not be harsh or judgemental if you made mistakes or failed to step into your highest self – treat yourself with compassion.

step 5: Repeat a nightly affirmation, releasing the energy of the day back into the universe (see page 154 for affirmations).

weekly ritual: sunday-night intention setting

step 1: Begin the ritual with some self-care, however you choose. This could be soaking in a bubble bath, taking a shower with nice lotions, taking some time to listen to your favourite music or make a nourishing meal. You could even take a walk in nature.

step 2: Then, when you're ready, choose a quiet place and time where you won't be disturbed. Light a candle or some incense to create a calming atmosphere.

step 3: Reflect on the past week, beginning with Monday. Celebrate your successes and note any lessons learned.

step 4: Set your intentions for the coming week. In your journal, write them down clearly, specifying what you want to achieve and how you want to feel.

step 5: Visualise each intention as if it has already happened. Feel the emotions of success and fulfilment. Know that you are embodying your highest self.

step 6: Close your ritual by saying, "I am ready to receive all the good this week has to offer."

monthly ritual: new-moon energy clearing

step 1: On the night of the new moon, create a space with candles, crystals (see page 184), or anything that feels special to you.

step 2: Take a few deep breaths to centre yourself. Express gratitude for the blessings of the past month and release this energy back into the universe.

step 3: Now turn to your journal and write down your goals and desires for the coming month. Be specific and detailed.

step 4: Close your eyes and meditate for a few minutes, visualizing your desires coming to fruition. Embody the joy and gratitude as if they have already manifested.

step 5: Add the written goals to your vision board or place them somewhere visible to remind you of your intentions throughout the month.

step 6: Thank the universe for its support and close your ritual by saying:

"I trust that everything I desire is on its way to me."

CRYSTALS

for

MANIFESTATION

In the realm of manifestation, crystals serve as powerful tools to amplify intentions, attract desired outcomes and harmonize energies.

Each crystal carries unique vibrations that align with various goals, such as abundance, love or spiritual growth.

By incorporating crystals into daily rituals, meditation or simply keeping them close, manifestors can enhance their focus, clarity and emotional well being.

When using crystals to amplify your manifestation, it is important to select a stone that resonates with a specific desire, set clear intentions and harness the crystal's natural energy to support these goals.

As symbols of nature's gifts, crystals remind us of the potential for transformation and the continuous flow of positive energy in our lives.

Read on to discover popular manifesting crystals and how they can resonate with your desires.

citrine / for abundance

Known as the merchant's stone, citrine is known for attracting wealth, success and prosperity. It is thought to enhance motivation, activate creativity and encourage self-expression, making it perfect for manifesting abundance and achieving personal goals.

clear quartz / the all-purpose manifestor

Also called the master healer, clear quartz amplifies energy and intention, helps to clarify your desires and expands your manifestation energy, making it an excellent all-purpose crystal for manifesting multiple goals.

rose quartz / for love

Possibly due to its lovely pinkish hue, rose quartz is intrinsically linked with love of all forms. Known as the crystal of unconditional love, rose quartz promotes all types of love, including self-love, and emotional healing as well as attracting loving relationships and harmonizing the energy around you to support emotional well being.

amethyst / for growth

While rose quartz is the stone of love, amethyst is the stone of emotional stability and growth. The purple crystal is known for enhancing spiritual growth, intuition, and clarity of mind. It also helps to clear negative thoughts and promote stillness, which aids in manifesting spiritual and personal growth.

green aventurine / for opportunity

In many cultures, the colour green represents good luck, and none more so than the green aventurine. Also called the stone of opportunity, green aventurine helps to manifest luck, wealth and success, thereby increasing an optimistic outlook and confidence in your own abilities.

pyrite / for motivation

While it may have earned the slightly unfortunate nickname of "fool's gold", pyrite's manifesting powers are not to be taken for granted. Pyrite is thought not only to represent abundance, prosperity, wealth and motivation but also to enhance willpower, perseverance and motivation.

carnelian / for confidence and creativity

This orange/red-toned stone represents warmth, strength and creativity as well as emotional balance and physical health. Carnelian stimulates motivation and courage in expression, helping to overcome self-doubt and procrastination.

selenite / for clarity

If you feel lost or uncertain in your manifestation, then invoke the power of selenite. Promoting clarity, peace and intuition, selenite clears energy blockages and enhances connections to the spiritual realm.

TO CONCLUDE

Ultimately, manifestation can be stripped back to the core tenets: We change our thoughts to change our behaviours and we change our actions to change our beliefs, we welcome the magic of manifestation into our lives.

It is energy, it is action, it is obvious and it is inexplicable.

are you ready for your journey?

We wish you well.